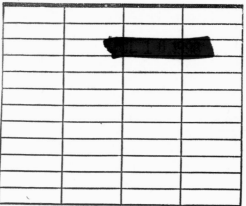

TRANSLATIONS

TRANSLATIONS

Charles Tomlinson

Oxford   New York

OXFORD UNIVERSITY PRESS

1983

Oxford University Press, Walton Street, Oxford OX2 6DP

London Glasgow New York Toronto
Delhi Bombay Calcutta Madras Karachi
Kuala Lumpur Singapore Hong Kong Tokyo
Nairobi Dar es Salaam Cape Town
Melbourne Auckland
and associated companies in
Beirut Berlin Ibadan Mexico City Nicosia

Oxford is a trade mark of Oxford University Press

English translations © Charles Tomlinson 1983

British Library Cataloguing in Publication Data
Translations
1. Poetry—Collections
I. Tomlinson, Charles
808.81 PN6101
ISBN 0-19-211958-3

Library of Congress Cataloging in Publication Data
Translations.
Selected poems, translated into English by Charles Tomlinson.
1. Poetry, Modern—19th century—Translations into
English. 2. Poetry, Modern—20th century—Translations
into English. 3. English poetry—Translations for
foreign languages. I. Tomlinson, Charles, 1927–
PN6101.T69 1983   808.81   83-4211
ISBN 0-19-211958-3

Set by Promenade Graphics Ltd.
Printed in Hong Kong

To Brenda

CONTENTS

INTRODUCTION

I HAVE been translating poems for more than twenty years and what follows represents a substantial selection from the total number. The first attempt was out of a language I did not know—Russian—and at the instigation of Henry Gifford who provided me with what he called transparencies. These consisted of the original texts, together with a literal interlinear translation and notes on usages and individual words. Poring over these thorough and sensitive aids, I had the illusion that I understood—if not Russian—the Russian of Tyutchev. The result was the least literal among my translations, because I could see no way of achieving a convincing tone of voice by a naked transposition of an original that owed so much of its force to a polysyllabic vocabulary and to nouns without articles. I had no illusions that if one stuck to Tyutchev's metre and rhymed in the same places that anything worth reading would necessarily be produced.

It was Henry Gifford who, as we proceeded with our work together, formulated a notion of poetic translation that arose from the immediate job in hand. This formulation has always stayed at the back of my mind in all subsequent undertakings. 'The aim of these translations', Gifford wrote, 'has been to preserve not the metre, but the movement of each poem: its flight, or track through the mind. Every real poem starts from a given ground and carries the reader to an unforeseen vantage-point, whence he views differently the landscape over which he has passed. What the translator must do is to recognize these two terminal points, and to connect them by a coherent flight. This will not be exactly the flight of his original, but no essential reach of the journey will have been left out ... Translation is resurrection, but not of the body.'

The handful of poems by Khodasévich was translated by what one might call our Tyutchev method; and we followed a similar method with Machado and Vallejo. To begin with, I could only read Spanish via Italian, the dictionary and a grammar, but eventually I learned it sufficiently to venture alone on my versions of Octavio Paz.

Octavio Paz, introducing his versions from several languages in *Versiones y Diversiones*, says of his own interest in translation that it is the result of passion and of chance. For me these two have often combined where I found that I had something in common with my original, or when I could learn something from him for my own poetic practice. On at least one occasion, the chance of coming upon a poet I wanted to translate, grew into the passion to do so, because of the very distance and difference of his work from anything I could have conceived of writing. This was the case when I first happened on some poems of Lucio Piccolo, led to them no doubt by the fact that I had been reading Lampedusa's *The Leopard*, and the discovery that these two were cousins. I had earlier gone to the poems of Ungaretti because they seemed to offer a parallel to William Carlos Williams' concern with the short line and the smaller syllabic components of verse, an interest I had long shared. Piccolo, on the other hand, although he could write compact lyrics, had the full baroque panoply of imagery, texture, rhymes in unexpected places and a syntax as intricate as his own mind. I suspect that some of my Italian friends even find him a little over-rich. For me he represented a challenge, part of which lay in the rhyming—a version of Piccolo without rhyme would be unthinkable—part in getting inside the skin of a twentieth-century Sicilian poet whose feudal background was both powerful and strange in the lithe density of its poetic embodiment.

In all these translations, such freedoms as I have taken with the original—and these have never been those of an imitation or adaptation—were to ensure a living result. As Sir John Denham wrote long ago: 'Poetry is of so subtile a spirit, that, in pouring out of one language into another, it will all evaporate; and, if a new spirit be not added in the transfusion, there will remain nothing but a caput mortuum.'

FYODOR TYUTCHEV

(1803–1873)

At Tegernsee

Lutherans, I admire your liturgy,
Taught by austerity
In word and stone,
By clean-swept space
Among the pious walls.

But girded to go
(Look), faith before you
Between the threshold and that emptiness
Pauses, her house deserted.

Girded to go,
She waits, the door unshut
But the hour sounding. Kneel now
And for your final prayer.

Sea and Rock

The sea, that leveller
Would have it down. Rebellion
Roars in the water now
That seethes and climbs, hisses
Against the untaken height.
Here, the devils' fires
Bubble Gehenna's cauldron, then
Up-end it, streaming.

Incessant on rock and shore
This bestial, bawling
Sibilance of the risen waves.
Mountain serenity, creation's
Sole giant contemporary
Stands over them, contained
In its pride of patience.

Mocked, they mass to regain,
Reclamber the granite sides
And howl their hopes
Into the teeth of stone, already torn
Turned by it backward
And the enfeebled onrush
Peters to turbid foam.

That space is small, measured
Against your waiting strength,
In which the sea must sicken
And the worn rollers, tamed
Make way for the spreading calm
And, uncomplaining, steal
Downwards to lick in peace your granite heel.

Sea Dream

A half sleep held me
While both sea and storm
Contended for our boat;
The waves' whim took
And two infinities
Played with me as they chose:
Around, the sound of rocks,
The clash and hissing
That sea-cymbals make
Impounded by them. Winds
Called to one another and the waves
Sang me to deafness. By chaos

Charmed, above the chaos
Rose my dream to where
It lightly lay, clear
To the pitch of pain and mute
On storm-crossed gloom.
Earth greened and ether shone
Taking the same contagion
From that fever. Gardens
In labyrinths, columns, palaces
Swarmed with a speechless throng
Of folk unknown, a mystery
Peopled by birds and flowers,
By beasts unnamed. I strode
My god's height and the world
Shone stilled beneath. But in these dreams
The ear caught ocean sounds,
And through the quiet of that altitude
Broke, like a shaman's cry,
The loud invasion of the waves and spray.

The Past

(Tsarskoe selo—site of the imperial palace)

Place has its undertone. Not all
Is sun and surface.
There, where across the calm
Gold roofs stream in,
The lake detains the image:
Presence of past,
Breath of the celebrated dead.

Beneath the sun-gold
Lake currents glint . . .
Past power, dreaming this trance of consummation,
Its sleep unbroken by
Voices of swans in passing agitation.

Neither Thought nor Threat

Neither thought nor threat
But a limp and sullen sleep
This night-sky gloom
Clouded from every quarter.
Only the intermittent flare as
Lightnings, deaf-mute demons
Converse with one another.

And now hangs lit
As by a pre-appointed sign
The whole stretch of sky,
Fields in the flash, far woods
Breaking from dark. They remerge
And the dark once more
Hushed, listens about them
As if it were aware
Of a decision taken
In the secret convocation
At the central height.

Spring

A formal Ode

Wrinkled, but not inured by years,
Deceived by men, unmanned by fate,
By all that subjugates the mind
Or leaves the heart disconsolate,
However you may bear defeat
Or wrongs, in recollection, sting—
What can withstand the subtle breath
And first encounter of the spring?

Her laws are wayward, self-decreed,
Winged visitant whom none may sue—
The hour appointed, she descends
Unconscious of your woes and you:
No wrinkle in that shining, calm
Forehead of immortality,
Whose lucence and indifference
Befit the brow of deity.

As though it were the first of springs,
She scatters round her fresh increase;
If other springs have ventured here,
No recollection breaks their peace:
She does not care: she only knows
These clouds are hers that sail so wide:
If flowers have shrivelled here before,
Her memory of that death has died.

Past being does not stir the rose
Nor Philomela with its fears;
Not for the past Aurora sheds
Her fragrant, aromatic tears;
Their life, an ocean without bound,
No dread of what is yet to be
Invades this present certitude
Diffused by every leaf and tree.

Accept the absolute decree.
The senses tell you of decay?
Plunge deeper than their knowledge dares
When deity has led the way:
Entering this reviving stream,
Wash wounds beneath the season's spate,
And, though they be the moment's gift,
Among these quickening joys participate.

The Fountain

Look. In a living cloud
The fountain hangs
Smoked round with spray.
How it shines, it burns—
Then breaks in a piecemeal mist,
A fire of dust—condemned
At the sacred precinct to these waste returns.

Eager anticipator!—
Thought, you are imaged in
This jet's defeat:
Your rise and your recall
Are measured here, and in these scattered beads
The expanse of sky that pre-ordains your fall.

Silentium!

Be silent, hide yourself:
In the still spirit
Hoard those hauntings
And let their coming
Be like the speechlessness of stars
By night-time waking, rising, homing.

What temerity may sound
Another's depth, survey its ground?
Utter your thoughts
They flow in lies. Dig down
You cloud the spring that feeds the silences.

Learn to live in yourself. There
Thought on thought,
Fretful of glare and stir,
Begets its untold transmutations
And their song
Only in silence may you hear.

18

A Storm, on the Road

The sun, unwilling and irresolute,
Looks fieldward. Listen:
A peal from the thunderhead. A passing
Frown on the earth's face.

Warm wind-gusts; the rain
Falling with hesitations; thunder
At a remove . . . Greening, the corn-crops
Under the storm loom greener.

There!—the blue of lightning
Cascades out of cloud, where fire
Distinct, white, flying
Has selvedged the borders.

Dust in a whirlwind flies
Upward, as the fields receive
The angrier force of drops
Enacting the thunder-threats.

From sun to field, once more
A misgiving glance:
And the whole earth, bewildered,
Drowns under radiance.

The Pacification

Storm ended. Still
(Blue-grey on rain-fresh green)
A smoke continued to uncurl
Out of the branches of the oak
Prone, where the lightning left it:
Songflow already brimmed
At covert crest, one foot
On foliage, a rainbow's arc
Poised there at rest.

Summer Storm

The dust sweeps by—summer
Rumbles in storm behind it,
Bursts out of ravaged clouds
To smear the blue, to charge
Impetuous on the wood, where tremors break
Loud in its stir and wilderness of leaves . . .

Wood giants bow
As if a heel, unseen
Had spurned them down.
Alarmed, their murmuring tops
Conspire for safety, while
Under unbroken birdsong
Through the sudden skirmish,
Spins to the road the first and yellow leaf . . .

Entering Autumn

Entering autumn, there ensues
(Its beauty is in brevity)
A season of crystalline repose,
Still day with lucent dusk . . .

Steady incursion of the blade
Lets space into the crop:
Emptiness over all, save where
Cobweb on idle furrow
Stretches its gleam of subtle hair.

Birdless, the vacant atmosphere;
But the first tempests lie
Folded, as liquid, mild
Warm-blue keeps winter from the resting field.

Let, Lord, Your Pity Fall

Let, Lord, your pity fall
On that man's lack,
Who, like the beggar,
Barred from garden graces
Carries the summer burning at his back.

The half-disclosures of the pale
Glance past his eyes
Where, cool and inaccessible,
Shadows of trees and valley grass
Spread through the parkland rural luxuries.

To gratify his need
The boughs prepare
No hospitality of shade,
And not for his refreshed delight
The fountain hangs its veil across the air.

Its fall of dewy dust
In cool profusion,
The grotto's blue
Beckon as from a cloud:
Let, Lord, your pity fall on his exclusion.

Night Takes the Distances

Night takes the distances
Ordained. And day, kind day
The comforter, must cede—
A dream dismissed, a gold cloth
Snatched aside that lay
On curtained chaos to supply our need:
The walls are down. All journeys lie
Through doors on dark that open into sky.
Orphaned by immensity,
Thought is homeless now as we:

No stay past self,
No bound where mind may bring
Its glow and gauge
As shapeless night unbars our heritage.

At Vshchizh

After the tumult and the blood
Had died, had dried,
Silence unmade its history:
A group of mounds; on them
A group of oaks. They spread
Their broad unmindful glories
Over the unheard rumour of those dead
And rustle there, rooted on ruin.
All nature's knowledge
Is to stay unknowing—
Ours, to confess confusion:
Dreamt-out by her,
Our years are apparitions in their coming-going.
Her random seed
Spread to their fruitless feat, she then
Regathers them
Into that peace all history must feed

On His Brother's Death

Journeying from your death
Towards my own,
This swept and sullen hill
Must be my halting place,
Vacancy, all beneath.

Alone. Yet for how long?
Small time will see
Emptiness dispossessing me
Of this deep night
And of the knowledge of my dispossession.

I, traceless, all will appear the same:
Night that is yet to be, sweep
Of the spreading steppe, snow
Howling where I had halted.

Brother, our selves and years
Were fellow-voyagers. Mine
Now wait in their fated turn,
Too poor for grief
Where time has uprooted them from living life.

To His Wife

Punishing God has taken all content
Of day and dark, of health and open air:
You he has left for my encouragement,
That, robbed of will, I am not robbed of prayer.

VLADISLAV KHODASÉVICH

(1886–1939)

Overstride, overspring,
Overfly, over—whatever you please—
But break out: stone from sling,
Star shooting the night skies . . .
You lost the thing—use your eyes now . . .

God only knows what you keep muttering,
Groping after your pince-nez, keys.

Lèdi kept washing and washing her hands,
Lèdi rubbed at them, tried to rub something out,
The memories of this *lèdi*
Gag on the thought of a bloodstained throat.

Lèdi, lèdi, like a bird
You writhe on your couch sleeplessly.
For three hundred years sleep has not come to you—
Nor for six years has it come to me.

It seemed an error to venture to English Khodasévich's mode of address for the wife
of the Thane of Cawdor.

24

The Blind Man

Feeling a way with his stick,
It is by guess the blind man wanders,
Cautiously setting down a foot
He ponders out loud.
And on the blind man's eyes
Crowds a whole world reflected:
House, meadow, paling, cow,
Shreds of blue out of the sky—
All that sight can never know.

Through light dank, drab, all winter-lack
—He bears a box, and she a sack—

Crossing a Paris paved in wet
Wife and her man with burdened step.

Behind them trailed my own footfall,
And then they reached the terminal,
For her, for him, silence was all.

You think for either words could be real?
A sack, a box all they could feel . . .
Heel clattering counterpointed heel.

ANTONIO MACHADO

(1875–1939)

Childhood Recollection

The schoolboys are at work.
Beyond the window panes
where day is raw and light is weak,
monotony of winter rain.

In the classroom. Pictured
on a placard there is Cain
in flight, and Abel, dead,
next to a scarlet stain.

Thin, ill-clad and dry as tinder,
the ageing master rumbles on
in a sonorous and hollow thunder;
the book lies open in his palm.

The chanting of the lesson, and
from a whole choir of children:
a thousand hundreds—a hundred thousand,
a thousand thousands make a million.

The schoolboys are at work.
Across the window panes
where day is raw and light is weak,
monotony of winter rain.

The Ilexes

Woods
    of Castilian ilexes
        on slope
and eminence
    hillsides
        and sudden fastnesses
woods, that
    dense with a brown and brambled dark
        are where
in the ilex tree
    strength and humility agree.
        As the axe
goes through
    fills you with empty space
        will no one
speak
    ilex trees
        to celebrate your qualities?
The oak is war
    the oak
        spells valour
mettle, rage immovable
    that writhes
        and ramifies—
a tree of caste
    that, thewed and ruggeder
        is more the master.
The tallness
    of the oak
        appears
to knot
    compress
        its hardiness,
an athlete who
    sinks his rooted weight into
        the soil below.

Pine is sea and sky
        and mountain:
                planet!
Palm:
        the desert,
                distance and the sun
the thirst, the cool
        spring we dream of in
                the rigid plain.
Who was it read
        in the legendary beech
                historic dread?—
battle
        crime,
                and who
has seen a beechwood in
        a forest full of pine
                and does not watch disquieted?
The poplars
        are the riverbank
                the lyres
of spring, beside
        the slow or swift-
                ly shifting flow
that spreads
        across the backwater
                or goes
contracted
        through tumultuous narrows.
                They imitate
in their eternal shivering
        the living waves
                of silver
at the river's spate.
        Elms
                in their parkland copses are
the good groves
        where
                Hope, bright-haired

must soon inherit
        the white
                of Contemplation.
The tree
        that bears it
                bears
the apple's scent;
        the aroma of its leaves
                cleaves
to the eucalyptus tree,
        to the orange
                fragrance of the flower;
and the garden's
        elegance is
                the dark unbending cypress's.
And you
        of the rustic stance?—
                the ashen trunk that has
neither grace nor arrogance
        and branches
                that are colourless;
'verdurous' would not
        describe your leaves
                (swart ilexes)
nor catch your vigour
        without strain and your
                humility that's firmness.
Nothing
        shines
                in the round
spread summit—
        neither
                your foliage
that's green-obscure
        nor the yellow green
                that marks your flower.
There's
        nothing
                handsome or superb

or warlike
    in your bearing,
        and in your mood
no petulance:
    erect, awry
        with that humility
that yields
    only to the law of life,
        you grow
and live
    the best
        that you know how.
The land itself
    was turned into
        a tree in you
brown ilex, burned
    by the sun
        and frost, by all
August and January
    can do,
        and you have stayed
constant
    beneath the snowflakes and the threads
        of rain,
made
    (as it were) a pact
        with the lands around
you, to remain
    impassive
        sound, serene
and sturdy—
    ever-green:
        and you have kept it
whether in Aragon
    and its marches, or
        where your darkness
perches on
    Pamplona's military peaks;
        and in

Extremadura,
    in Castile
        our Spain's
creator,
    on level
        ridge and mountain—
the plateau
    encircled by
        a youthful Duero
and along
    the snaking Tagus through
        Toledan land
and where
    in Santandér
        your way draws seaward.
A frank
    frown of Castile
        your dissonance was heard
in Moorish Córdoba,
    and you are there
        wooding Madrid,
stately and sombre
    in the chill
        of Guadarrama,
Castile's disdain
    that must correct
        the vanity, display
and fever
    that infect the court:
        I know
how the most distinguished
    brushes have painted you
        complete with greyhounds
and with chargers, how
    Augustan poets
        sang
and royal huntsmen made
    you deaf with muskets: you
        however, are the field

and hearth
    the tutelary shade
        of the good villagers
who wear
    brown serge
        and cut for brands
your branches with their naked hands.

Summer Night

Beautiful
    the summer night:
        fronting the rectangular
deserted, ample
    village square,
        tall houses
stand,
    their balconies
        unshuttered that command
a prospect of stone benches
    of acacia and spindle-trees
        that trace
symmetrically black
    their shadows
        on the white of sand.
Moon
    in the zenith,
        in the tower
the clock's
    illumined sphere.
        And I
in this old village
    pass alone,
        am phantomed by
its sharpness
    its solidity.

To a Dry Elm

Sparsely
    with a few green leaves
        the old elm
breaks:
    lightning, rot
        could not gainsay
what rains of April
    sun of May
        at last bring out.
A century
    it's held the height
        above the Duero.
Moss-stain spreads
    a yellow on the white
        bark of its dusty trunk
the worm invades.
    Unlike the poplars
        singing guardians
of road and river
    it will never be
        to the tawny nightingales
their nesting tree.
    In file
        the military ants
go climbing over it:
    within
        the grey webs thicken as
the spiders spin.
    Before the woodman fells
        and you
are turned into
    a beam to stay a bell
        a shaft, a yoke,
before
    tomorrow when
        you'll smoke and redden

33

on a wretched, wayside
     hovel hearth,
          before
the whirlwind tear your roots
     or breath
          of white sierras
rend you or river
     send
          through gulch and valley to the sea
let me record
     this growing beauty branches stored:
          for how the heart
must read
     in what it sees
          its expectations'
life and light
     and echoing
          await
a second miracle of spring!

Poem of a Day

Rural Meditations

Behold me
     here—the nightingales'
          apprentice, master
of *la gaya scienza*
     formerly:
          I teach
the living tongues
     to a damp and bleak
          sombre and straggling
village that belongs
     half to La Mancha, half
          to Andalusia.

Winter:
    the fireside:
        in the street
a fine rain falls
    alternately as mist or sleet.
        I
a husbandman in fancy
    dream of fields.
        O Lord,
how well thou dost
    and how
        it rains!
on vineyards and on olive-groves
    fields of barley and of beans:
        a still
a small and steady rain.
        How the sowers of the grain
            will bless
like me
    your bounteousness,
        and those who live
by gathering
    the olive,
        those who hope
for the fortune of a meal
    and have
        all that they own
in the year's deceitful wheel—
    this
        and every year that's gone.
Rain,
    rain on!
        and alternate
as mist or sleet
    and then again
        reverting to a tenuous rain
rain, Lord, rain!
    My chamber keeps
        a wintry light:

the afternoon
    through rain and glass
        sifts its grey illumination—
a medium where thoughts may pass.
    The clock
        neglected in its corner
looms distinct:
    its tick
        forgotten in its repetitions
now beats on
    within my consciousness
        and boring, bored
a uniform metallic heart
    speaks its one and only part:
        tick
tock:
    in villages like these
        does one catch
the pulse of time?
    Truceless
        before the clock
one, rather, fights
    against monotony
        that, in these villages
alights
    to measure
        the passage of their vacancies.
But, clock, is yours
    this time of mine—
        are mine your hours?
(Tick, tick)
    There was a day
        (tick, tick) that passed
and that which I
    most loved
        death made away.
A knell from far
    fades
        into the rain's

minute, untroubled chime
    that rings against the window panes.
        A husbandman in fancy
I
    return to fields.
        Lord,
how they'll bless
    your bounteousness—
        those
who sow the bread.
    Lord,
        is not the rain you bring
law in the ox-ploughed field
    and in
        the palace of the King?
Bounteous water,
    leave
        behind you life—
you that go
    drop by drop, and
        spring by spring
and river upon river flow,
    that, like this time
        of weariness supply
the sea
    with transitory life,
        with all that seeks nativity
to germinate
    to spring
        and be.
Be
    merciful
        for you become
tomorrow's
    early ear of grain, and
        you restore
tint in the field
    and in the flesh
        and more:

reason
>madness
>>bitterness
the grief that wishes for
>and yet remains unsatisfied
>>with all belief.
Dark
>is coming down;
>>the wire
reddens within the bulb,
>gathering to a glow
>>with scarce more show
than wax on a lucifer.
>God only knows
>>where (under these tomes, reviews
and scribblings)—
>ah, here they are:
>>my spectacles.
New books.
>One
>>I open
by Unamuno.
>Oh, the chosen
>>cherished spirit
of the Spain that shall inherit
>our coming life
>>our resurrection!
This
>teacher of a country school,
>>unheard of,
he knows no defection,
>Rector of Salamanca!
>>Yours—
the philosophy you call
>dilettante and inconstant
>>balanced
upon its slender rope—
>nourishes, great
>>Don Miguel

his buried hope.
    Water
        of the good spring,
fugitive
    always; always living;
        poetry—
that cordial thing.
    Architectonic?
        (Do you look
for architecture
    in the wind,
        in the soul's structure?)
Rower,
    sailor
        across that sea
which has no shore.
    Henri Bergson:
        Les données
immédiates
    de la conscience.
    Is this
another Gallic artifice?
    This Bergson
        is a sell—agreed,
Maestro Don Miguel?
    He's no Immanuel Kant—
        it's the immortal somersault
his writings want;
    this devilishly clever Jew
        locates
free will
    within his mind's own gates.
        Ah, well—
every wise man has his problem,
    every idiot his theme.
        And yet
it still would seem
    to matter whether
        we, in a short and evil life

shall live
      as either slaves or free.
            But if
(as the poet shows)
      it's seaward all our living flows—
            all will come
to the same thing.
      Oh, these villages!
            reflections
readings
      annotations
            soon will end
in what they are:
      the yawns
            of Solomon.
Is it all
      solitude of solitudes
            vanity of vanities
as saith Ecclesiastes?
      My waterproof,
            umbrella
and sombrero:
      the rain is moderating—
            shall we go?
Night:
      the talk is on
            in the rear room
at the apothecary's
      where they define
            what makes the liberals such swine
and Don José
      scents consolation
            in the return (predicted)
of the conservative administration,
      all spicing it
            from the inexhaustible resources
of a people's wit:
      'The past
            and future

are the same.
    Others
        like us, will blame
the government.
    All changes,
        comes
and goes.' And then,
    for arbitration:
        'No evil lasts a century
to plague a nation.'
    'And the beans
        have come on splendidly—'
'These rains—'
    'The barley—'
        'And they'll flower
by March
    unless the frost—'
        'The labourers
will count the cost
    in sweat—'
        'Torrents—'
'Seas
    would scarcely quench the thirst of olive trees.'
        'In other days—'
'The rain would rain
    at the Lord's will, then
        as now.' 'Until
tomorrow, gentlemen.'
    Tick
        tock
tick-tock: one
    day has gone
        like any other
says the monotone of the clock.
    My table bears
        les données de la conscience
immédiates.
    It's adequate
        this I

41

that's fundamental
        and at times
                creative and original, that
mingling in mortality
        its freedom and contingency,
                can feel
can see, and yet
        must overleap the confines
                of its narrow keep.

Baeza, 1913

Lament of the Virtues and
Verses on account of
the Death of Don Guido

It was pneumonia
finally carried away
Don Guido, and so the bells
(*din-dan*) toll for him the whole day.

Died Don Guido
gentleman; when younger
great at gallantry and roistering,
a minor talent in the bullring—
older, his prayers grew longer.

This Sevillan gentleman
kept (so they say)
a seraglio, was apt
at managing a horse
and a master
at cooling manzanilla.

When his riches dwindled
it was his obsession
to think that he ought to think
of settling in quiet possession.

And he settled
in a very Spanish way
which was—to marry
a maiden of large fortune
and to repaint his blazons,
to refer to the traditions of
'this house of ours',
setting a measure
to scandals and amours
and damping down the expenditure on pleasure.

He became, great pagan
that he was,
brother in a fraternity;
on Holy Thursday could be seen
disguised
(the immense candle in his hand)
in the long robe of a Nazarene.
Today
you may hear the bell
say that the good Don Guido
with solemn face
tomorrow must go
the slow road to the burial place.

For ever and for always
gone, good Don Guido . . .
'What have you left?' some will say—
I ask, 'What have you taken
to the world in which you are today?'
Your love for braid
and for silks and gold
and the blood of bulls and the fume that rolled
from off the altars?

To good Don Guido and his equipage
bon voyage!

The here
and the there,
cavalier,
show in your withered face,
confess the infinite:
the nothingness.

O the thin cheeks
yellow
and the eyelids, wax,
and the delicate skull
on the bed's pillow!

O end of an aristocracy!
The beard on breast
lies limp and hoary,
in the rough serge
of a monk he's dressed;
crossed, the hands that cannot stir
and the Andalusian gentleman
on his best behaviour.

The Ephemeral Past

Habitué of a small-town club, this man
who saw Carancha poised one day
to take the bull,
has a withered skin, hair going grey,
eyes dim with disenchantment, and beneath
the grey moustache, lips bent
in nausea and a look
that's sad—yet sadness it is not
but something more, and less: the void
of the world in the hollow of his head. He still
sports a jacket coloured currant-red

44

in a three-pile velvet, breeches
booted at their extremities and a caramel
Córdoba hat, turned and furbished well.
Three times he inherited, then lost the lot
three times at cards and twice
was widowed. An illegal round of chance
alone will make him brighten
sprawled at the green baize table;
once more the blood begins to flow
as he recollects a gambler's luck
or the afternoon of some torero,
drinks in an episode from the life
of a daring bandit of the road
or the bloody prowess of a knife.
He satirizes with a yawn the government's
reactionary politics and then
predicts the liberals will come to power
again, just as the stork returns to the bell-tower.
Something of a farmer still, he eyes
the heavens, fears them and at times will sigh
thinking of his olives and, disconsolate,
watches for weather-signs when rain is late.
For the rest, boredom. Taciturn, hypochondriac,
shut in the Arcadia of the present,
and to his brow
only the movement of the smoke gives now
its look of thought. This man is neither
of yesterday nor tomorrow
but of never. Hispanic stock, he's not
the fruit that grew to ripen or to rot,
but shadow-fruit
from a Spain that did not come to be,
that passed away, yet, dead,
persists to haunt us with a greying head.

To José María Palacio

Palacio,
    good friend,
        is spring
already clothing
    the branches of the poplar trees
        on road and river?
In the plain
    of the upper Duero
        spring
comes so slowly
    but when she comes
        she is all sweetness! . . .
The old elms,
    have they
        any new leaves?
As yet
    the acacias will be bare,
        and under snow
the mountains of the sierras.
    Oh, there
        in the sky of Aragon
the so beautiful
    white and rose
        mass of Moncayo!
Are the thorns
    in flower among grey rocks
    and are
white daisies there
    in the delicate grass?
        By now
storks will have been
    arriving on those belfries.
        There will be
greens of the coming wheat,
    a going
        of brown mules

into fields prepared for sowing
and of the peasants
who plant late crops
with the rains of April.
Already
bees
will broach
the thyme and rosemary.
Are plum trees
into blossom, do
violets
remain there too?
Stealthy,
with lures for the partridge
under a length of cloak,
huntsmen will not be absent.
Palacio,
good friend,
do the riverbanks
hold nightingales already?
On a blue
afternoon, the first
roses and first lilies
in the gardens,
go
climb Espino:
airy Espino where *her* country is.

To the Young Thinker
José Ortega y Gasset

The laurel and the ivy wreath!
to you, the gods' elect
must fall
(Sophia's architect)
this coronal.
Chisel, hammer, stone
and masons serve you!

May cold Guadarrama's peaks
to you alone
who, sombre, think a new Escurial
proffer their deepest blue of all.
And may the austere Philip loom
to bless beside his royal grave
tomorrow's architecture
and the progeny that Luther gave.

Lines to a Master

Professor, not of energy
Francisco de Icaza
but of melancholy.

II

An ancient stem
transmits his brevity of word
his depth of apophthegm.

III

He's like the olive grove:
small shade beneath,
all fruit above.

IV

In his clear verse, you'll hear
both thought and song
flow without fret or fear

V

And in perfect rhyme
—thus the river's two-fold poplar
at the water's brim.

VI

His cantos bear
water of standing pools,
stillness unyielding there.

And yet it does:
certain and seawards,
without haste it goes.

VII

His songs possess
(present gist of old affections)
aromas and aloe's bitterness.

And from the favour
of the Indian sun
fruit in ripeness and rich savour.

VIII

Francisco de Icaza, you
who span two Spains—
the Old and New,

a hundred réal piece must hold
beside your lyre
your viceroy's profile cut in gold.

CÉSAR VALLEJO

(1895–1937)

Trilce III*

The grown-ups
what time are they coming back?
Blind Santiago is striking six
and already it's very dark.

She'd soon be home, mother said.

Aguedita, Nativa, Miguel,
watch out, don't go there where
griefs that double you up
have just gone by
whining their memories
towards the silent yard
and where the hens are still
getting settled, they were so scared.
Better if we stayed
here: she'd soon be home, mother said.

Besides, we should not
grieve. Let's go on
seeing the boats (mine's
the nicest of the lot!)

* 'For "trilce" Vallejo compounded two numerals, *trillón* and *trece*, a trillion and thirteen. A truncated trillion is held prisoner by the ill-chanced and broken thirteen. Or perhaps, like the arm of the Venus de Milo in another *Trilce* poem (not represented here), it should be seen rather as uncreated, subject to the "perennial imperfection" of life.'—Henry Gifford.

with which we play
the whole blessed day without a quarrel
as good children should: they've stayed
in the puddle, ready,
freighted with sweet things for tomorrow.

Obedient and resigned,
let's wait like this
for the return, the excuses
from the grown-ups—they
always the first to abandon
the small ones in the house,
as if it were us were unable to get away.

Aguedita, Nativa, Miguel?
I'm calling, feeling about
in the dark for you.   Don't
go out and leave me
and I the only one shut in.

Trilce XV

In that corner
      where we slept together
so many nights, I have sat down
to travel now. They have taken away
the bedstead of the dead bridal pair
or who can say
what might have happened!

Early, to other occupations
on you went and now exist
no more. It is the corner where
one night, between your tender punctuations
I read beside you
a tale of Daudet's. It is the beloved
corner. As to that, why argue?

I have set myself to recall
the finished days of summer,
your entrance and your exit,
sufficient and pale and small
through the rooms.

In this night of rain, now far
from both the two, I leap up
suddenly and there are
two doors opening shutting
two doors which go
        and come in the wind
shadow   to   shadow.

Trilce XXIII

Glowing bakehouse of those my biscuits, pure
innumerable yolk of childhood, mother. O your four

birds' meals, astoundingly ill-bewailed
mother: your beggars. The last two
sisters, Miguel who died and me
still tugging a tress for each letter of the abc.

Morning and afternoon, in the upstairs
parlour, you doled us out shares
twice over, of time's rich
communion wafers, so that we
might have left to us
husks of watches, stopped punctually
in the going-round of the twenty-four.

Mother, and now! Now
in what small cavity would remain,
in what capillary shoot, a certain crumb
tied now to my throat
that doesn't want to go down. Now
that even your pure bones will become

flour, that there will be
nothing in which to knead,
tender honeyjar of loving-kindness!
even in the crude shadow, even in the big molar whose gum
throbs from that little milky recess
that carves itself forth and buds
unnoticed—you saw it so many times!—
in the closed hands newly born.

So the earth will hear
in your taciturnity, how they all
come collecting from us the rent of the world
where you leave us, and the price
of that interminable bread. And they
collect it from us, when we
being little then (as you would see)
could have snatched it away
from no one; when you gave it to us . . .
can you say
        little mother?

Trilce XXVIII

I have eaten my dinner alone now, and have not been through
mother, or may I, or help yourself, or water, or father who
in the eloquent offertory of corn-on-the-cob, should ask
to cover up his slowness in getting round
to the image he wants, the larger links of sound.

How could I go to eat. How was I to help myself
to those things from such distant dishes when
my own hearth will have been broken
and to my lips no mother reveals herself either.
How was I to make a meal on almost nothing.

I have dined at the table of a good friend,
with his father just arrived from the world,
with his grey aunts who speak
in thrush-coloured retouching of porcelain,
sibilant through all their widowed gaps;
and with free places for cheerful wind-instruments
because they are in their own house. And a fine thing too!
And I have ached with the knives
of this table my whole palate through.

To eat from these tables thus, at which you feel
an alien love instead of a love your own,
changes to earth the mouthful which does not toast the

MOTHER,

makes a blow of the bolus that won't go down,
turns the sweet to gall, and coffee to funeral oil, when
at last your own hearth has been broken,
and the maternal help-yourself emerges no more from the
tomb,
the kitchen in darkness, the poverty of love.

Trilce LII

And we shall get up whenever the inclination
takes us, although Mamá, all ablaze
awakes us with a songbird burst
of lovely maternal rage. And we
shall laugh at this on the sly
biting the top
of the warm vicuña blankets: And just you stop
misbehaving!

The smoke from the Indian huts ah! little outflung
branching vagabonds! they'd get up early to play
at bluish kites bluestaining;
and, soiling hearthstones and ornamental
roofs, would bring our way

54

the exciting smell of cowdung,
        to fetch us out into
the childish air which doesn't know
its letters yet, to fight
there, for the string of the kites.

Another day, you will graze
between your omphaloid hollows
        avid caves
        ninth months
        curtains-across-my-stage.

Or you will want to go with the old folk
to lay bare the watermain of a twilight,
so that by day may rise up
all the water that passes by night.

And you get there
dying of laughter and at the musical feast,
parched popcorn, flour with butter
(with butter!); you seize by the hair
the sprawling *peon* who today
forgets once more
to say his *buenos días*,
those *días* of his, *buenos* with the *b*
of a layabout which insist
on backfiring out of the poor devil from the behind
of the dentilabial *v*
that sentries his mind.

Trilce LVIII

In the cell, in the solid, even the corners
huddle up. I set to rights

The stripped men, who crumple
submit, become rags.

I climb from the horse
panting and snorting lines
of blows and horizons; one
lathery foot against three hooves.
And I help him: Come on,
you creature!

Less. One would take
always less of what it befell me to divide
in the cell, in the liquid.

My prison companion
was eating wheat from the slopes
with my own spoon,
when, at my parents' table, a child
I fell asleep chewing.

I prompt him: go on
back round the other corner:
go quickly . . . go now . . . go soon!

Heedlessly, I
find him his reasons, plan:
there's room
for a bit of a bed in here
merciful, rickety. No doubt of it
that doctor was a sound man.

I'll laugh no more
when my mother prays
in childhood and on Sunday
and at four
of an early morning
for wayfarers, for prisoners,
sick
and poor.

In the sheepfold of boys, no more I'll
deal blows at any
who afterwards would cry
still bleeding: Another Saturday
I'll give you my cold meat
only don't beat me.
All I'd say to him now is: O.K.

In the cell, in the gas unlimited
till it grows round in condensation,
who stumbles outside?

Trilce LXI

I get down
        from the horse tonight,
before the door of the house, where
at cockcrow I took my leave.
It's shut and nobody answers there.

The stone bench, astraddle on which
Mother gave birth
to my elder brother
so that he might saddle
loins I had ridden bareback
by village lanes
and by garden walls, a child
of the village; the bench on which
I left to yellow in the sun
my painful childhood . . . And this
pain that imprints the title page?

A god in the alien peace,
the brute sneezes
as if also calling out;
it noses about
striking the pavement.

Soon, fears
make it hesitate; it neighs,
twitches alert ears.

Father must be awake
praying, and will think perhaps
I have been out late. My sisters
humming their illusions
simple, ebullient
in their work for the approaching feast
and now, almost nothing
is wanting. I wait
I wait, my heart
an egg in its moment
that obstructs itself.

Numerous family that we left
not long since,
nobody is keeping
watch today and not one
candle set on the altar
for our homecoming.

I call again . . . nothing.
Silent, we begin sobbing and the beast
neighs, neighs all the more:

They are all asleep for ever,
and so soundly
that, in the end, my horse
gets weary in turn
of nodding his head, and between
sleep lets fall
at each nod that it's all
right, everything
is all right.

Trilce LXV

Mother, tomorrow I'm going
to Santiago, to steep myself in your blessing
and your lament. I am arranging
my disillusions and the flush
on the wound of all my false to-ing and fro-ing.

Waiting for me,
there will be your arch of surprise, the shorn
columns of your disquietudes will arise
that bring life to its bourne. Waiting, the patio's there,
the downstair corridor with its round
mouldings and festive borders.
Waiting for me will be my tutor chair—
good and bulky and large-of-jaw,
a piece in dynastic leather
which stops anymore
groanmoaning at the buttocks as great-great-grandsons
shift from one thong to another.

I am sifting my purest affections. I am windlassing—
can't you hear
the plummet heaving, the irregular
chopping of reveille sounds?
I am moulding your formula of love
for every hollow of this ground.

Oh, if the tacit wheels
would dispose themselves for all
the most distant belts,
for whatever encounters may befall.

So, dead immortal. So.
Under the double arches of your blood,
where one must pass so much on tiptoe
that even my father, to go that way
humbled himself to less than half a man to be
the first little one you had.

59

So, dead immortal.
Between the colonnade of your bones which cannot fall
even in weeping, and in whose side
even Destiny cannot
slide one of his fingers.
So dead immortal.
So.

Trilce LXVI

Tolls
     the second day of November.
These chairs are good welcomes.
The bough of presentiment
goes, comes
rises, undulates sweating
weighed down in this drawing room.   Sad
tolls the second day of November.

Deadmen, what your gone teeth do
cut through below, as you
stitch up blind nerves, unmindful there
of the hard fibre
rotund singing workmen repair
with inexhaustible hemp, the knots
throbbing innumerably
at crossroads.

You, deadmen with shining knees, pure
by dint of yielding yourselves, how you
saw the other heart through
with your white crowns meagre
in cordiality.   Yes.
             You:
                 the dead.

Sad tolls the second day of November.
And the bough of presentiment is
bitten by a cart, that simply
rolls down the street.

Trilce LXXVII

It hails and with so much zest
as if it wanted to have me wake
and augment the pearls that I gather
from the very snout of each tempest.

Let it not dry up, this rain.
Grant me this grace at least
to fall in its place now,
or that they might lay me in earth
soaked in the water
that would spout from all the fires.

How far will it reach into me, this rain?
I am afraid I shall be left with some flank dry;
I am afraid it will go away without having proved me
in the droughts of incredible vocal cords,
by which
to harmonize,
one must rise always—never descend!
(Don't we rise perhaps to go down?)

Sing, rain, along that coast that still no seas attend!

OCTAVIO PAZ

(born 1914)

Dawn

Cold rapid hands
Draw back one by one
The bandages of dark
I open my eyes
                Still
I am living
            At the centre
Of a wound still fresh

Here

My steps along this street
Resound
            In another street
In which
            I hear my steps
Passing along this street
In which

Only the mist is real

Oracle

The cold lips of the night
Utter a word
Column of grief
No word but stone
No stone but shadow
Vaporous thought
Through my vaporous lips real water
Word of truth
Reason behind my errors
If it is death only through that do I live
If it is solitude I speak in serving it
It is memory and I remember nothing
I do not know what it says and I trust myself to it
How to know oneself living
How to forget one's knowing
Time that half-opens the eyelids
And sees us, letting itself be seen

Friendship

It is the awaited hour
Over the table falls
Interminably
The lamp's spread hair
Night turns the window to immensity
There is no one here
Presence without name surrounds me

Touch

My hands
Open the curtains of your being
Clothe you in a further nudity
Uncover the bodies of your body
My hands
Invent another body for your body

Certainty

If it is real the white
Light from this lamp, real
The writing hand, are they
Real, the eyes looking at what I write?

From one word to the other
What I say vanishes.
I know that I am alive
Between two parentheses

Landscape

Rock and precipice,
More time than stone, this
Timeless matter.

Through its cicatrices
Falls without moving
Perpetual virgin water.

Immensity reposes here
Rock on rock,
Rocks over air.

The world's manifest
As it is: a sun
Immobile, in the abyss.

Scale of vertigo:
The crags weigh
No more than our shadows.

Ustica

The successive suns of summer,
The succession of the sun and of its summers,
All the suns,
The sole, the sol of sols
Now become
Obstinate and tawny bone,
Darkness-before-the-storm
Of matter cooled.

Fist of stone,
Pine-cone of lava,
Ossuary,
Not earth
Nor island either,
Rock off a rock-face,
Hard peach,
Sun-drop petrified.

Through the nights one hears
The breathing of cisterns,
The panting of fresh water
Troubled by the sea.
The hour is late and the light, greening.
The obscure body of the wine
Asleep in jars
Is a darker and cooler sun.

Here the rose of the depths
Is a candelabrum of pinkish veins
Kindled on the sea-bed.
Ashore, the sun extinguishes it,
Pale, chalky lace
As if desire were worked by death.

Cliffs the colour of sulphur,
High austere stones.
You are beside me.
Your thoughts are black and golden.
To extend a hand
Is to gather a cluster of truths intact.
Below, between sparkling rocks
Goes and comes
A sea full of arms.
Vertigoes. The light hurls itself headlong.
I looked you in the face,
I saw into the abyss:
Mortality is transparency.

Ossuary: paradise:
Our roots, knotted
In sex, in the undone mouth
Of the buried Mother.
Incestuous trees
That maintain
A garden on the dead's domain.

The Mausoleum of Humayun

To the debate of wasps
The dialectic of monkeys
Twitterings of statistics
It opposes
                    (High flame of rose
Formed out of stone and air and birds
Time in repose above the water)

Silence's architecture

In the Gardens of the Lodi

Into the total blue
The domes of the mausolea
—Dark, shut round on their own thoughts—
Suddenly send forth
                    Birds

Tomb of the Poet

The book
         The glass
The green obscurely a stalk
                          The record
Sleeping beauty in her bed of music
Things drowned in their names
To say them with the eyes
                          In a beyond I cannot tell where
Nail them down
                     Lamp pencil portrait
This that I see
                 To nail it down
Like a living temple
                     Plant it
Like a tree
          A god
Crown it
         With a name
                      Immortal
Derisible crown of thorns
                          Speech!
The stalk and its imminent flower
                               Sun-sex-sun
The flower without shadow
                          In a beyond without where
Opens
      Like the horizon
                       Opens
Immaculate extension
Transparency which sustains things
Fallen
       Raised up
By the glance
               Held
                     In a reflection
Moons multiplied
                  Across the steppe

Bundle of worlds
                        Instants
Glowing bunches
Moving forests of stars
Wandering syllables
Millennia of sand endlessly falling away
                                    Tide
All the time of time
                        TO BE
A second's fraction
                    Lamp pencil portrait
In a here I cannot tell where
                        A name
Begins
        Seize on it, plant, say it
Like a wood that thinks
                        Flesh it
A lineage begins
                In a name
An adam
            Like a living temple
Name without shadow
                        Nailed
Like a god
            In this here-without-where
Speech!
            I cease in its beginning
In this that I say
                I cease
TO BE
        Shadow of an instantaneous name

I SHALL NEVER KNOW MY BOND'S UNDOING

One and the Same

(Anton Webern, 1883–1945)

Spaces
      Space
Without centre no above or below
Devours and engenders itself and does not cease
Whirlpool space
               And it falls into height
Spaces
      Clarities
Cut into jewel-points
                Hanging
From night's sheerness
Black gardens of rock crystal
Flowering along a bough of smoke
White gardens that explode in air
Spaces
      A sole space that unfolds
Flower-face
          And dissolves
Space into space
All is nowhere
Place of impalpable nuptials

Bird's Eye View
To Guillermo Sucre

Furiously
        It whirls round
Over a reflection
               Falls
In a straight line
                  Clear-cut
Whiteness
           Ascends
The beak now blood-red
Scattered salt
              Scarcely a line
As it falls
          Straight
Your glance
           Over this page
Dissolved

White and Black Stone

Sima*
      sows a stone
in the air
         the stone rises
Inside
       there is an old man sleeping
If he opens his eyes
             the stone explodes
whirlwind of beaks and wings
                on a woman
who flows away
         among the beards of autumn
The stone descends
           burns

* Sima: painter, Czech by birth.

71

in the plaza of the eye
                        flowers
in the palm of your hand
                            speaks
hanging
        between your breasts
languages of water
                    The stone ripens
Inside
    the seeds are singing
                        They are seven
Seven sisters
            seven vipers
Seven drops of jade
                    seven words
asleep
    in a riverbed of glass
Seven veins of water
                    in the centre
of the stone
            that the glance breaks open

GUILLAUME APOLLINAIRE

(1880–1918)

Rhenish Winter

In the house
   of the vine-grower
      women were sewing
Lenchen
   pile up the stove
      put on
water for the coffee
   —Now that the cat
      has thawed itself
it stretches-out flat
   —Banns are in
      at last for Gertrude
and Martin her neighbour
The blind nightingale
   essayed a song
but quailed in its cage
   as the screech-owl wailed
      The cypress out there
has the air of the pope
   setting out in snow
      —That's the post
has stopped for a chat
   with the new schoolmaster
      —This winter is bitter
the wine
   will taste all the better
      —The sexton
the deaf and lame one
   is dying
      —The daughter

of the old burgomaster
    is working
        a stole in embroidery
for the priest's birthday
    Out there
        thanks to the wind
the forest gave forth
    with its grave organ voice
        Dreamy Herr Traum
turned up with his sister
    Frau Sorge
        unexpectedly
Mended
    you call these
        stockings mended Käthe
Bring
    the coffee the butter the spread
        bread in Set
the jam and the lard and
    don't forget milk
        —Lenchen
a little more
    of that coffee please
        —You could imagine
that what the wind says
    was in Latin
        —A little more
Lenchen
    —Are you sad
        Lotte my dear
I think
    she's sweet on somebody
        —God
keep her clear
    of that—As for me
        I love nobody
but myself—Gently
    gently
        grandmother's telling her rosary

—I need
    sugar candy
        I've a cough Leni
—There's Paul
    off with his ferret
        hunting for rabbits
The wind
    blew on the firs
        till they danced in a ring
Love makes
    a poor thing of Lotte
        Ilse
isn't life bright
    In the snarled stems
        the night
was turning the vineyards
    to charnels of snow
        shrouds
lay there unfolded
    curs
        bayed at cold travellers
He's dead
    listen
        from the church
the low bell-tone
    The sexton had gone
        Lise
the stove's dwindled to nothing
    rekindle it
        The women
made the sign of the cross
    and the night
        abolished their outline.

GIACOMO LEOPARDI

(1798–1837)

On a May Night

After the prose of Leopardi's journal

Gloom in my mind: I leaned
at a window that showed the square:
two youths on the grass-grown
steps before the abandoned church
fooling and falling around
sat there beneath the lamp: appears
the first firefly of that year:
and one of them's up already
to set on it: I ask
within myself mercy for the poor thing
urging it *Go go* but he
battered and beat it low then turned
back to his friend: meantime
the coachman's daughter
comes up to a window
to wash a platter
and turning tells those within
Tonight it will rain
no matter what: it's as black
as the inside of a hat
and then the light at that
window vanishes: the firefly
in the interval has come round:
I wanted to—but that youth
found it was moving turned
swore and another
blow laid out the creature
and with his foot he made

a shining streak of it
across the dust until
he'd rubbed it out: arrived
a third youth from an alley-way
fronting the church
who was kicking the stones and
muttering: the killer laughingly
leaps at him bringing him down
then lifts him bodily:
as the game goes on
the din dies but the loud
laughs come volleying through:
I heard the soft voice
of a woman I neither knew nor saw:
Let's go Natalino: it's late:
For godsake he replies
it isn't daybreak yet: I heard
a child that must surely be
hers and carried by her
babblingly rehearse
in a milky voice
inarticulate laughing sounds
just now and then out of its own
quite separate universe: the fun
flares up again: *Is there any*
wine to spare at Girolamo's?
they ask of someone passing:
wine there was none:
the woman began laughing softly
trying out
proverbs that might fit
the situation: and yet that wine
was not for her and that
money would be
coin purloined from the family
by her husband:
and every so often she
repeated with a laughing patience
her hint *Let's go*

in vain: at last a cry
Oh look comes from them
it's raining: it was a light spring rain:
and all withdrew bound homewards:
you could hear the sound
of doors of bolts
and this scene
which pleased drawing me from myself
appeased me.

GUIDO GOZZANO

(1883–1916)

Winter Piece

'. . . cree . . . ee . . . ee . . . ee . . . eak . . .':
                         the spreading fracture
arabesqued the ice: strident, it seems it lives.
'Back to the edge!' Each one of them arrives
safe by the brink, beyond the insecure
abandoned crust. 'The edge!' One breath of fear
disperses the brigade of fugitives.

'Stay here!' I felt her fingers interlace
my own in living links, my arm in custody
as she entwined it: 'Stay, if you love me!'
And on that cunning and deserted glass
we sped alone in wide and winging grace,
deaf to their shouts, drunk with the immensity.

Ghostlike and gliding there with all weight gone,
robbed of my past, robbed of my memory,
two minds abandoned in a single folly,
we cut enormous circles on the pane.
Creak, said the split ice in a duller tone . . .
Creak with a groan of darker melancholy . . .

At which I shuddered, and like one who hears
the shrill and laughing mockery of Death,
stared down with eyes intent and saw beneath
two faces through transparency appear,
livid as though we stretched out on a bier . . .
Creak, from the ice, as with a deeper breath . . .

79

Oh how, bound by those fingers, could I doubt,
or how could world and comfort signify?
O voice of instinct, your imperious shout,
O fleshly wish to live eternally!
My fingers from her fingers tearing free,
panting and overcome, I scrambled out . . .

Alone, she stayed on, circling wide across
her solitary realm, ignored her name;
decided to return, in her own time,
laughing approached with wind-dishevelled tress,
and fluttering, beautifully fearless,
swept in like a stormy petrel where she came.

She passed the flock of females, as uncaring
for their admonishment as their alarm;
sought for and found me standing in a swarm
of friends, and joined me courteously laughing:
'Belovèd sir, I thank you!' offering
her small hand to me as she hissed—'You worm!'

GIUSEPPE UNGARETTI

(1888–1970)

Tedium

Even tonight will pass

This going round and round in solitude
irresolute shadow of the tram-wires
on the wet asphalt

I watch the heads of the cabmen
in half-sleep
wavering

In Memory

He was called
Mohammed Sceab

A descendant
of nomad emirs
a suicide
because he no longer had
a homeland

He loved France
and changed his name

Became Marcel
but was not French
and could no more
live
in the tents of his people

where one can
listen to the cantilena of the Koran
sipping coffee

And he could not
raise
the song
of his desolation

I accompanied his coffin
together with the woman who kept
the hotel where we lived
in Paris
at 5 rue des Carmes
a run-down sloping alley

He rests
in the graveyard at Ivry
suburb that has the look
always
of the day
when a
fair breaks up

And perhaps only I
still know
he lived

Vigil

A whole night through
flung down beside
a comrade
slaughtered
his mouth
grimacing
turned to the full moon
his stiffened
hands
penetrating
into my silence
I wrote
letters full of love

Never have I
clung so
close to life

Rivers

I lean on this mutilated tree
abandoned in this defile
that has the slow
quiet of a circus
before the show or after it
and I watch
the unhurried transit
of clouds crossing the moon

This morning I lay down
stretched in an urn of water
and as if I were a reliquary
reposed there

The Isonzo scurrying by
polished me
like one of its stones

I lifted
my four limbs up
and went off
like an acrobat
over the water

I squatted
close by my clothes
filthy with war
and like a bedouin
bowed down to receive
the sun

This is the Isonzo
and here I came
to know myself better
for the docile fibre
of the universe that I am

My torment
is when
I do not believe myself
in harmony

But those secret
hands
that knead me
confer
a rare
felicity

I have passed once more
through the phases
of my life

These
are my rivers

This is the Serchio
from which perhaps

two millennia
of my peasant people
my father and my mother
have drawn their water

This is the Nile
that saw me
born and grow and
burn for the want of knowledge
in the wide plains

This is the Seine
and in her turbid flow
my elements were mixed anew
and I began to know myself

These are my rivers
told over in the Isonzo

This is my nostalgia
which from each
one shines
through to me
now that it is night
and my life shows
like a corolla
of shadows

Transfiguration

I stand
my back to a tumulus
of bronzed hay

A sharp pang
bursts seethes-in
from the fat furrows

Well-born I feel myself
of folk with land

I feel myself in the eyes
of him who follows
the sky's phases
a man wrinkled
like the bark
on the mulberry trees he's pruning

I feel myself
in the children's faces
a rosy fruit
red-glowing
through trees whose foliage is shed

Like a cloud
I distil
as the sun warms

I feel myself
being spread in a kiss
that consumes me
and calms

Vanity

Suddenly
there towers
above the rubble
the limpid
wonder
of immensity

86

And the man
bent
over the sun-
startled water
comes to
as a shadow

Rocked and
softly
shattered

Wanderer

In not one
spot
of earth
can I
settle and stay on

With each
new
region
that I reach
I find myself
wearied
at having been
bored before
by the very
scene's familiarity

And I break out of it always
an alien

Born
returning from epochs too
lived-through

To relish the contént
of a sole minute
of initial life

I look
for a country that is innocent

Soldiers

One fares as
in autumn
on the trees
the leaves do

Brothers

From what regiment are you
brothers?

Tremulous word
in the night

Leaf scarce born

In the pain-racked air
involuntary recoil
of man confronting his
fragility

Brothers

End of Cronus

The terrified hour
In the womb of the firmament
Wanders alien

A soot
The colour of lilac crowns the mountains,

It was the last cry to lose itself.

Innumerable Penelopes, stars,

Again the Lord gathers you to him!

(Ah, blindness!
Landslide of nights . . .)

And he puts back Olympus,
Eternal flower of sleep.

Cain

He runs over the fabulous sands
And his foot is nimble.

O shepherd of wolves,
Your teeth are of the brief light whose goad
Bites into our days.

Terrors, impetuous rage,
Death-rattle of the forest, that hand
That shatters at a single stroke old oak trees,
You are made in the heart's image.

And when it is deepest darkness,
Are you the delighted body
Among spell-bound trees?

And as I burst with longing,
The mood changes, suspicious you veer away,
With my own step you evade me.

Oh to sleep like a spring of water in the shade!

Then when the morning is hidden still,
You would be lifted, soul
On the calm and welcome of a wave.

Soul, shall I never pacify you?

Shall I never see in the night of my blood?

Boredom's daughter, incapable of secrets,
Memory, incessant memory,
Is there no wind to carry away
The clouds of your dust?

My eyes would return to me in innocence,
Perpetual springtime I should see

And, new at last,
You would be honest, memory.

You Were Shattered

I

The countless, ruthless, scattered stones of grey
Still quivering in hidden slings
Of smothered flames of origin
Or with the terrors of virgin torrents
Ruining down in implacable caresses,
—Rigid above the dazzle of the sand
Across a deserted skyline, do you not remember?

And the slope, which opened to the only
Gathering of shade within the valley—

A sand-pine, stretched yearning and gigantic,
Twisted into lone fibres of steep flintstone
Stubborner than the other damned,
Cool the maw full of butterflies and grasses
Where it split from its roots,
—Do you not remember it raving mute
Held by a massive pebble's sphere
In a perfect balance
Suddenly and magically there?

From branch to branch light wren
Avid eyes drunk with wonder
You gained its speckled summit,
Rash small singer,
Only to glimpse once more in the lucid deep
Of a bed and tranquil chasm of the sea
Fabulous turtles
Amid the algae rousing up from sleep.

The furthest stretch of naked nature
And its subaqueous pomps
Funereal admonitions.

2

You lifted your arms like wings
And brought the wind to birth once more
Running through the weight of the unmoving air.

None ever saw your light foot
Have done with dancing.

3
Glad grace,
How should you not be shattered
In so impenetrable a blindness
You simple breath and crystal,

Gleam too human for the unpitying,
Shaggy, furious, droning
Roar of a naked sun.

Little Monologue

Under the rinds of trees, as through a vacancy,
Streams of sap, astir already
And unknotting, wind
In a delirium of branches-to-be-budded:
Uneasy in his sleep, winter
Telling February the reason
Why it must stay short; and moody
Though he may be, he is no longer
Secretively cheerless. As if
Over some biblical calamity,
To all appearances the drop lifts
Along a shore which from that moment
Seeks to repopulate itself:
From time to time, abrupt, re-emerging
Tower follows tower;
In search of Ararat once more
Wanders the ark, afloat through solitudes;
They are climbing up to limewash the dovecotes.
Snow shifts from over the bramble stocks
Across Maremma
And
Near and far, a continuous
Cheeping whispering spreads through the air
Where birds brood;
Speeding from Foggia
To Lucera the car
Disquiets with its headlamps
Foals in their stalls;
In Corsica's mountains, at Vivario,
Men sitting out the night about the fire
Under the room's kerosene light,
With blanched and shaggy beards
Above hands heavy on sticks,
Chewing unhurried pipes, they are listening
To Ors' Antone sing
Accompanied by the murmur of the *rivérgola*

Vibrating between the teeth
Of the boy Ghiuvanni:

Your field's as thick with clover
As my sky is clouded over

Outside a trampling of feet
Looms louder, mingled with the howls and gurgling
Of swine they bring to be butchered, and butchered
They are, for tomorrow
Carnival begins, and still
Through the windless air it goes on snowing.
Forsaken; behind three
Minute parish churches,
Assembled in ranks across the slope
Roofs red with tiles
The newest houses
And,
Covered in washing
The oldest almost invisible
In the confusion of the dawn;
The fragrant forest
Of Vizzavona is crossed
Without our ever being aware through the windows
Of its larches save for their trunks,
And seen only in scraps,
And
There is the time
We climbed from the east through mountains
And the windings meandered even in the driver's voice:

There was sun here, there shadow, shadow there,

On he follows, repeating it to himself
And whether east or west
Always mountains, and worse—
Where the knot of mountains begins to alternate—
The spread of seclusion:
Is there no term to the tedium of it?

And,
At more than a thousand
Feet the car takes for its track
A road hacked through the chain
Narrow, icy
Leaning over the chasm.
The sky is a sky of sapphire
And wears that clear colour
Which in this month belongs there,
February colour,
Colour of hope.
Down, down until it reaches
To Ajaccio, such a sky
As numbs one but not because it is cold,
Because it is sibylline.
Down, down the unending
Incline until it encompasses
A dark sea in whose
Hidden windings a continual
Roaring is stifled:
And the Neptunia advances:
It sails on into Pernambuco
And,
Alongside rocking skiffs,
And hesitant lighters
Over the lustre and elasticity of the water
Black, it imposes on the tiny port
Its neat profile's elegant bulk.
Everywhere, up ships' stairs,
Through crammed streets,
On the steps of trams,
One meets with nothing that is not dancing
Whether thing, beast or person,
Day and night, and night
And day, because it is Carnival.
But at night they dance best,
When, dark's antagonists,
Between sky and ground, hail down
From the whirling of fireworks, flowers of fire—

Accomplices of the night,
Multiplying its ambiguities,
Speckling the livid sea.
All are suffocating with heat.
The equator is a couple of steps away.
Hardship harried the man from Europe
Who must accustom himself
To the upside-down seasons,
And, above all,
By mixing his blood:
Is not February the month for grafting?
And still more did he suffer
When his blood turned mulatto
In that accursed coupling
Of human souls with the labour of slaves;
But, on southern ground,
He found at last
He could dress up those dog days
In his own most unexpected mask.
And now he will never cease to charm
This false February
And,
Putrid with sweat and stench,
Rolling their eyes they dance without pause
Raucously, unendingly singing
With the intent ingenuousness of the place:

O irony, irony
Was all he used to say.

Recollection is the sign of age
And today I have recalled
A few halting places in my long stay
On earth that fell in February,
Because in February, I grow
More watchful than in other months
For what may follow.
I am more bound to it
Than to my own life

By a birth
And by a grief;
But now is not the time to speak of that.
And in this month I too was born.
It was stormy, rain never ceased
That night in Alexandria.
The Shi'ite Moslems were holding their festival
Of moon amulets:
A child on a white horse gallops by
And the people throng around him
Drawn spell-bound into the circle of prophecy.
Like Adam and Eve they seem, stupefied
By the fate which has tied them to the earth:
Ear sharpens now
For divinations,
And a woman out of the mob of Arabs
Rears up, gesticulates where
Lightning on a rock has clawed a form,
And with foaming mouth bears witness:

A mahdi, still shapeless in the granite
Is outlining the grasp of his terrible arm;

But my mother, woman
Of Lucca that she is,
Laughs at such tidings
And with a proverb replies:

If in February each pathway's awash, that's sure sign
It is plumping the cobbles with oil and with wine.

Poets, poets, we have put on
All the masks; yet one
Is merely one's own self.
With terrible impatience
In that vacancy of nature
Which falls every year in February, we have set
For ourselves a limit on the calendar:

The day of Candlemas
With the re-emergence from shadow
Weak tremor of tiny flames
Where small candles burn
Of unpurified wax,
And the day, after some weeks,
Of *Thou art dust and unto dust thou shalt return*;
In the vacancy, and because of our impatience
To emerge from it,
Each one, and we
Old men too with our regrets,
And none knows
Unless he prove it for himself
How illusion can
Throttle a man
Who lives by regret alone;
Impatient in the vacancy, each one
Raves, futile, wears himself out
To be reborn in some fantasy,
Which will also be vain,
And terror comes of it,
Time is too swift varying its deceits,
That we should ever take warning from it.
Dreams should be fit
Only for boys: they possess
The grace of candour
That heals after all corruptions, once it renews
Or changes at a breath the voices within.
But why boyhood
And suddenly recollection?
There is nothing, there is nothing else on earth
But a gleam of truth
And the dust's vacuity,
Even if, with incorrigible madness
The living man seems to strain
Toward the lightning flash of mirages
In innermost depth and deed
Again and again.

LUCIO PICCOLO

(1901–1969)

Veneris Venefica Agrestis

She springs from the ground-clinging thicket, her face
—gay now, now surly—bound in a black
kerchief, a shrivelled chestnut it seems: no fine fleece
the hair that falls loose, but a lock
of curling goat-hair; when she goes by
(is she standing or bending?) her gnarled and dark
foot is a root that suddenly juts from the earth and walks.
　　Be watchful she does not offer you her cup of bark,
its water root-flavoured that tastes of the viscid leaf,
either mulberry or sorb-apple, woodland fruit that flatters with lies
the lips but the tongue ties.
　　She governs it seems
the force of rounding moons
that swells out the rinds of trees
and alternates the invincible ferments,
flow of the sap and of the seas. . . .
　　Pronubial, she, like the birds that bring
seeds from afar: arcane
the breeds that come of her grafting.
　　And the mud walls of the unstable
cottage where the nettle grows
with gigantic stalk, are her realms of shadows:
she ignites the kindlings in the furnaces of fable.
　　And round the door, from neighbouring orchard ground
the fumes that rise
are the fine, unwinding muslins of her sibiline vespers.
　　She appears in the guise
of the centipede among the darknesses
by water-wheels that turn
no more in the maidenhair fern.

She is the mask that beckons
and disappears, when the light
of the halfspent wicks
makes voracious the shadows in the room where
they are milling by night, working at the presses,
and odours of crushed olives are in the air,
kindled vapours of grapejuice; and lanterns come
swayed to the steps of hobnailed boots.
    The gestures of those who labour
in the fields, are accomplices
in the plots she weaves:
the stoop of those who gather up dry leaves
and acorns . . . and the shoeless tread and measured bearing
under burdened head, when you cannot see
the brow or the olives of the eyes
but only the lively mouth . . . the dress
swathes tight the flanks, the breasts, and has comeliness—
passing the bough she leaves behind
an odour of parching . . .
or the gesture that raises the crock
renewed at the basin of the spring.
    She bends, drawing a circle:
her sign sends forth
the primordial torrent out of the fearful earth
(and the foot that presses the irrigated furrow
and the hand that lifts
the spade—power of a different desire summons them now);
she draws strength
from the breaths of the enclosures,
the diffused cries, the damp and burning
straw of the litters, the blackened
branches of the vine, and the shadow that gives back
the smell of harnesses of rope and sack,
damp baskets, where who stands
on the threshold can descry
the stilled millstone, hoes long used to the grip of rural hands:
the rustic shade ferments with ancestral longings.
    Rockroses, thistles, pulicaria, calaminths—scents
that seem fresh and aromatic, are

99

(should your wariness pall) the lures
of a spiral that winds-in all,
(night bites into silver
free of all alloy of sidereal ray) she will
blur in a fume of dust the gentle hill-curve.
   Now, she's in daylight, one hand against an oak,
the other hangs loose—filthy and coaxing,
her dress black as a flue-brush . . .
and the sudden rush of wind
over the headland, sets at large
and floods with blue
a tangle of leaves and flourishing bough.
   She promises, too, discloses the ardour
freshness, vigour of the breath that frees
peach and the bitter-sweet
odour of the flowering almond tree; under coarse leaf
are fleshy and violent mouths, wild offshoots,
between the ferns' long fans
obscure hints of mushroom growths,
uncertain glances of water glint through the clovers,
and a sense of bare
original clay is there
near where the poplar wakes unslakeable thirst
with its rustling mirages of streams
and makes itself a mirror of each breeze,
where, in the hill's shade,
steep sloping,
the valley grows
narrow and closes
in the mouth of a spring
among delicate mosses.
   If, for a moment,
cloud comes to rest
over the hill-crest or the valley threshold,
in the living shade
the shaft of that plough now shows
which shakes which caresses unleafs
the bush and the forest rose.

The Night

Sometimes the night turns gentle;
if it can raise from the obscure ring
of mountains a breath of freshness
to bring suffocation to an end, from the walls nearby
it releases a cluster of songs, it rises
with the creepers through the long arches, on the high
terraces, on the great pergolas,
in the openwork of the unstill branches, it reveals
carnations of gold, it gathers
faint secrets from the threads of water on the gravel beds
or takes tired steps
where the dark waves smash against breakwaters of white.

Suddenly on the screen of dreams
it blows into living veins faces already ash, words
that are voiceless . . . sets spinning the girandole of shadows:
on the threshold, above, all around
a vain emptiness, a vast passageway sways into forms,
a moving glance seizes
and a glance that stops cancels them.

Reverberations of echoes, shatterings, insatiate memories,
re-flux of lived-out life that gushes over
from the urn of Time, the hostile waterclock
that breaks into pieces; it is a mouth of air
that furiously feels for a kiss,
a hand of wind that wishes for a caress.

On the stone flights, on the step of slate,
at the door that is splitting with dryness,
the quiet oil is the sole light;
little by little, the rigour of the sung verses
spent, the dark is more dense—it seems like rest
but it is fever; the shadow hangs from the secret
beating of an immense
Heart
      of
          fire.

Landscape

Above the roof
ascends, impends all at once
the mountain—to the left, encumbered
with a thorny green on green, with blankets
of a shed leafage, agèd tree-rinds, brush:
and caper, euphorbia hang at the winds'
mercy; where the coastline bends
and summons the shadow in, spreading it across
the scape of wrinklings, at the slope's
summit, folds fall open: valleys
of thicker green, there you can seek
and find puffball, buttercup and wild leek:
on dense leaf, on creeping bronchia
scum, wood spit, dark dew
of the swollen stalk, the thorn, the goitred
and oozing stem, that which remains
clammy with rainbow-coloured stains, which never sees
sunlight (and assiduously the invisible shuttles
weave, mutate, but the cycle will stay
the same forever) fed with an ancient moisture,
a mildew of vegetation . . .
and perhaps an eyeless lizard slides away . . .

(From *Anna Perenna*)

Under a Bourbon King

What days those were! and little was enough to make
story and fable flourish, and the lip
was prompt, the ear attentive amid the suspense
of faces. The word was a sprig of corn in the wind
dense with grains that the air
scattered to perplexed city, to somnolent village,
to far-off cottages.
The skein-winder of the hours
reeled-round times of quiet expectation,

cool returns to the vast divans of patterned flowers.
St Elmo's fire spelled safety
in the seastorm and the serene Bear
came back to shine
tiptoeing on the sea
before the beacon-lights, before the dark
irresolution of the further coastline.

Terror along the shore: the fury of rape
drags off amid shrieks a skirt for a flag
and the corsair, with his black-porcelain eyes,
his serpentine beard:
scimitar strident against peasant arms, rage
replies from the hillside fort, from slit and parapet
the mortar bragging its force in bursts of fire,
thundering away like a fair-day drum from its stage.
Then, it's as if the sound
of the tumult brings-out a more vast dead calm:
the irrigation water spreads
evening into the plots of garden ground.

Unstill Universe

Unstill universe of gusts
of rays, of hours without colour, of perennial
transits, vain displays
of cloud: an instant and—
look, the changed forms
blaze out, millennia grow unstable.
And the arch of the low door and the step
worn by too many winters, are a fable
in the unforeseen burst from the March sun.

ATTILIO BERTOLUCCI

(born 1911)

Solo

In September here the sun burns on
a candle near to its consummation
the meadow I cross regaining level ground
is an altar whose cloth is one of grass.

Saffrons needle it through with their lilac incarnate
it is bordered by thorns of the Lord and by
those of that cursed property the times humiliate
beneath agriculture's slow decay.

Berries bloodstain it ready in advance
for the autumn season it takes a softer tone
from the dog-rose with its vegetable coral
and the tuft that circles and tightens around the nut of the hazel.

Can I be preacher impromptu—a calling deferred—
to say mass at the impious noonday hour
on this natural table of spacious apennine—
offering up this flesh and blood of mine

to the asses lizards and butterflies in pairs
sole witnesses for the deserted benches where women prayed
of my faith and my unquiet beatitude—
while the plane that carries the mail is drawing away and spins

a wool which in the distance spread out in sunlight scintillates?

Giovanni Diodati

My astonishment almost felicity
when I discovered Giovanni Diodati—
whose protestant Bible which I was reading
somehow entered my household—Catholic

if only tepidly with tenacious roots—
was the friend of that John Milton
whom today—late—I count among those poets
I care for most. The shimmer

of his lines—when he depicts Eve naked
garnishing a cloth
with reddening fruits in the autumn
of Paradise its noonday corruscating

at the guest's approach—Raphael
the Archangel—for a meal for three—
isn't it just the same as in the prose
of the exile from Lucca beside Lake Leman

where the Bride of the Canticle appears
suggesting to the intent adolescent—
fiery twilight coming slantwise in
to the resonant granary of wheat
hiding-place in air vertigo

of a plain black with swallows—the saliva of kisses?

NOTES ON THE POETS

FYODOR TYUTCHEV (1803–73)

Tyutchev's first published poem was an imitation of Horace, though Horatian is the last adjective one might think of applying to the precursor of the Russian symbolists, of Blok and Pasternak. However, translation played an important part in the literary evolution of this restless and tormented man: he was Heine's first Russian translator and he did versions also of Goethe, Schiller and Lenau. Pushkin, Turgenev and Tolstoy all admired his work, and Lenin is said to have kept a volume of it on his desk. Tyutchev's poetry, with its evocation of summer storms, sea, light, silence, is true to the quality of the present moment as it reveals itself in the landscape and in the mind.

VLADISLAV KHODASÉVICH (1886–1939)

Khodasévich left Russia in 1922 with Pushkin's works in eight volumes in his knapsack. He was not rehabilitated in the USSR until 1963. The complete literary man—poet, essayist, critic, biographer, translator—he writes a prose and verse that is at once lucid and compact. Paris, the scene of his poverty in exile, saw also the partial destruction of his archive by the German authorities in 1942. One of the few sources of information in English about this important but little known figure is Nina Berberova's *The Italics Are Mine*. The author was his wife.

ANTONIO MACHADO (1875–1939)

Machado was a poet of the Castilian landscape and of the tragic sense of life as experienced in a Spain that had seemingly cut itself off from the rest of Europe. He died as a refugee in France after the defeat of the Republic which he supported. Of an older generation than Lorca and Alberti, he lacks their welter of unexpected imagery and claims 'merely [to] cut ancient roses from Ronsard's garden'. This is clearly an exaggeration: his sobriety and straightforwardness could only have occurred in the twentieth century and there is still much to be learned from them in both Spain and Latin America.

CÉSAR VALLEJO (1895–1937)

Vallejo, a Peruvian, seems to have invented surrealist poetry before the event. But the leaps and apparently free associations of his verse address themselves to a consistency and solidity of theme and content which surrealist poetry (Aimé Césaire is one of the great exceptions) often seems to want. The poems from *Trilce* (1922), translated here, arose from the period he spent in a Peruvian jail where, in his helplessness, he felt his way back to childhood and to a sense of the vulnerability of humanity in general. He died in France, a supporter of the Spanish Republic.

OCTAVIO PAZ (b. 1914)

Paz's poetry, unlike that of too many Latin American writers, looks as much to Europe and the Golden Age of Spain, to Quevedo and Góngora, as to native sources. In many ways he is the political conscience of Mexico. His many prose books and essays, his work as editor of *Plural* (suppressed) and *Vuelta* (still active), are the measure of this fact. For many years a diplomat, he has been back in Mexico City since 1971. 'Poetry is the *other* voice,' he has written, 'Not the voice of history or of anti-history, but the voice which, in history, is always saying something different.'

GUILLAUME APOLLINAIRE (1880–1918)

Guillaume Albert Wladimir Alexandre Apollinaire Kostrowitzky, illegitimate son of Mlle Olga de Kostrowitzky and an officer in the Bourbon army, Francesco Flugi d'Aspermont, was born in Rome, but grew up French. The friend of painters (there are portraits by Picasso and De Chirico), he wrote as a propagandist for cubism. His collage poems pre-date those of Pound and Eliot. Having survived serious shell injuries in the 1914 war, he succumbed to the post-war influenza epidemic.

GIACOMO LEOPARDI (1798–1837)

My one example of Leopardi is not from the great poetry of the *Canti*. Indeed, it was not, to begin with, 'poetry' at all, but an extract from his notebooks, with which I have attempted an experiment. Had Leopardi been born a century later, might he not have cast these incidents as a poem? In his superb *Il sabato del villaggio*, he comes close to doing something like what I mean, though even there he does not allow the criss-cross of overheard conversation and the weave of desultory events to suggest the music and movement of his poem in quite the twentieth-century way I had in mind. Yet the possibility is wholly implicit in the prose passage which I have paced as verse.

GUIDO GOZZANO (1883–1916)

Gozzano is a kind of Italian Laforgue. He, too, died young of consumption, was an ironist and came early into his powers. He lacks Laforgue's capacity to create new forms of a kind Eliot and Pound were to find so decisive in their development. But there is a warmth and humanity in his work which perhaps Laforgue never attained, and a mastery of touch in the ripple and flow of his carefully rhymed stanzas which playfully set off the conversational and fragmented elements of daily life that they contain.

GIUSEPPI UNGARETTI (1888–1970)

Ungaretti, pulling against the current of d'Annunzian heroics, attempted in his early work something similar to that reconstitution of the strength of the syllable and the short verse line such as one finds in Pound and Williams. Prompted by the experiments of his friend Apollinaire, Ungaretti brings much weight to bear on the single word, holding word and cadence tightly to the design of the unfolding poem. The brilliant Marxist critic and poet, Edoardo Sanguineti has complained, with some justice, that after these beginnings, Ungaretti, via what he himself calls 'fabulous illumination and myth', reinstates 'the Petrarch–Leopardi axis'. Sanguineti implies that the anguish and religiosity of the later work is a touch willed and that there is reason to prefer Ungaretti's moment of setting out, the moment of the 'parola tremante/nella notte'.

LUCIO PICCOLO (1901–69)

Cousin of Giuseppe di Lampedusa (author of *The Leopard*), Lucio Piccolo, Baron of Calanovella, also explores the 'strong if languid pull of the Sicilian earth', the sudden violences of weather, the world of old baroque palaces and churches. Piccolo is less of a realist than his cousin and has described himself as 'a disciple of Yeats, Baudelaire, Mallarmé'. His are the poems of an entropic history that can only consume, a history turning itself into fable where the Moorish predators of Sicily become 'the Moorish band of winds'. Montale, introducing Piccolo's work, situates the poetry's technical strength in its 'lean, intense and wiry diction'.

ATTILIO BERTOLUCCI (b. 1911)

Bertolucci is poet, journalist and art-historian. His late poetry, of which two examples are included here, goes from strength to strength, and the long-delayed 'novel' in verse, of which only fragments have appeared to date, promises to be a work of great originality. Some of the poems seem to combine the retrospective glance of a Thomas Hardy with the syntactical complications of a Proust, and both these authors are among Bertolucci's enthusiasms. He has also translated Edward Thomas.

ACKNOWLEDGEMENTS

SOME of the materials of this book have appeared previously in *Versions from Fyodor Tyutchev* (1960), *Castilian Ilexes* (1963), *Ten Versions from Trilce* (1970), *Selected Poems of Octavio Paz* (1979), and in the following periodicals: *The Critical Quarterly, Delos, Listen, The Nation, National Review, New Mexico Quarterly, The Nonesuch Magazine, Poetry* (Chicago), *Poetry Nation Review, Spectrum, Stand, The Times Literary Supplement.* It was in *The Hudson Review* that the following first appearances occurred: Machado's 'The Ilexes', 'Poem of a Day' (vol. xv, no. 2); Piccolo's 'Veneris Venefica Agrestis', 'The Night', 'Landscape', 'Under a Bourbon King' (vol. xx, no. 3); Paz's 'Tomb of the Poet', 'Ustica', 'Touch', 'Friendship', 'Dawn', 'Oracle', 'Certainty' (vol. xxi, no. 3); Ungaretti's 'Little Monologue' (vol. xxiii, no. 1).